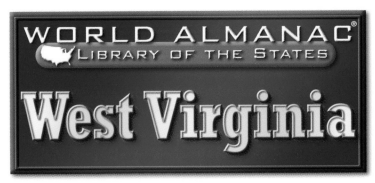

THE MOUNTAIN STATE

by Justine Fontes and Ron Fontes

WORLD ALMANAC® LIBRARY

Please visit our web site at: www.worldalmanaclibrary.com
For a free color catalog describing World Almanac® Library's list of high-quality books
and multimedia programs, call 1-800-848-2928 (USA) or 1-800-387-3178 (Canada).
World Almanac® Library's fax: (414) 332-3567.

Library of Congress Cataloging-in-Publication Data available upon request
from publisher. Fax (414) 336-0157 for the attention of the Publishing
Records Department.

ISBN 0-8368-5163-3 (lib. bdg.)
ISBN 0-8368-5334-2 (softcover)

First published in 2003 by
World Almanac® Library
330 West Olive Street, Suite 100
Milwaukee, WI 53212 USA

Copyright © 2003 by World Almanac® Library.

A Creative Media Applications Production
Design: Alan Barnett, Inc.
Copy editor: Laurie Lieb
Fact checker: Joan Verniero
Photo researcher: Annette Cyr
World Almanac® Library project editor: Tim Paulson
World Almanac® Library editors: Mary Dykstra, Gustav Gedatus, Jacqueline Laks Gorman,
 Lyman Lyons
World Almanac® Library art direction: Tammy Gruenewald
World Almanac® Library graphic designers: Scott M. Krall, Melissa Valuch

Photo credits: pp. 4-5, 6 © West Virginia Division of Tourism/Stephen J. Shaluta; p. 6 © ArtToday;
p. 6 © West Virginia Division of Tourism/David E. Fattaleh; p. 7 © West Virginia Division of
Tourism/Stephen J. Shaluta; p. 7 © West Virginia Division of Tourism; p. 9 © West Virginia Division
of Tourism/Stephen J. Shaluta; p. 10 © North Wind Picture Archives; p. 11 © North Wind Picture
Archives; p. 12 © AP/Wide World Photos; p. 13 © West Virginia Division of Tourism/Stephen J.
Shaluta; p. 14 © North Wind Picture Archives; p. 15 © West Virginia Division of Tourism; p. 17
© West Virginia Division of Tourism/Stephen J. Shaluta; p. 18 © West Virginia Division of
Tourism/Stephen J. Shaluta; p. 19 © Hulton Archive/Getty Images; p. 20 (left) © West Virginia
Division of Tourism/David E. Fattaleh; p. 20 (center, right) © West Virginia Division of Tourism/Stephen
J. Shaluta; p. 21 (left, right) © West Virginia Division of Tourism/Stephen J. Shaluta; pp. 21 (center),
23 © West Virginia Division of Tourism/David E. Fattaleh; p. 26 © Roger Ressmeyer/CORBIS; pp. 27,
29 © West Virginia Division of Tourism/Stephen J. Shaluta; p. 31 © Getty Images; p. 31 © AP/Wide
World Photos; p. 32 © West Virginia Division of Tourism/David E. Fattaleh; p. 33 © West Virginia
Division of Tourism/Stephen J. Shaluta; p. 34 © West Virginia Division of Tourism/Stephen J. Shaluta;
p. 35 © West Virginia Division of Tourism/David E. Fattaleh; p. 36 © AP/Wide World Photos; p. 37
(both) © AP/Wide World Photos; p. 39 © Hulton Archive/Getty Images; p. 40 (top) © Hulton
Archive/Getty Images; p. 40 (bottom) © Hulton Archive/Getty Images; p. 41 © AP/Wide World
Photos; pp. 42-43 © North Wind Picture Archives; p. 44 (both) © West Virginia Division of
Tourism/Stephen J. Shaluta; p. 45 (both) © West Virginia Division of Tourism/David E. Fattaleh

Printed in the United States of America

1 2 3 4 5 6 7 8 9 07 06 05 04 03

West Virginia

For Purple Mountain Majesties...

— *"America the Beautiful" by Katharine Lee Bates*

West Virginia's nickname, the Mountain State, refers to the Appalachian Mountains, which contain West Virginia completely. The mountains are more than a place to ski or shoot rapids. They are home to wildlife and a hard-to-reach sanctuary where traditional ways are preserved right along with the jarred peaches.

The mountains do not provide an easy living. West Virginians are hard workers who farm steep hillsides, dig dangerous, underground coal mines, or shape molten glass before blazing furnaces. Many are descended from poor Scottish, Irish, and German immigrants who were glad to have a piece of land to call their own — even if it was as steep as a ladder. These settlers not only worked hard, but also celebrated life with bluegrass music and dance.

West Virginia's formal names tell another part of the state's story. When the people of Virginia's western counties decided to form their own state in 1861, they called it *Kanawha*, Native American for "place of the white rock." The "white rock" was salt, which Native Americans had taken from the natural brine pools and which is now harvested for the state's chemical industry.

The people of Kanawha soon changed the name to West Virginia. This name reflects the state's political history, including its determination to stay in the Union instead of joining the Confederacy. The people's political outlook was more Northern (antislavery) than Southern, since the western part of the state was too hilly for the big farms that used slaves.

Perhaps the nickname says it best. West Virginia is the Mountain State, rugged and wild — not an easy place to live, but a good one. Mountaineers know their legs may be tired by the end of the hike, but the sunset will be worth it.

▶ Map of West Virginia showing the interstate highway system, as well as major cities and waterways.

▼ The spectacular Dolly Sods Wilderness has high valleys, rolling hills, beautiful waterfalls, and swimming holes for campers. Its location in the Monongahela National Forest is perfect for berry picking, hiking, and sightseeing.

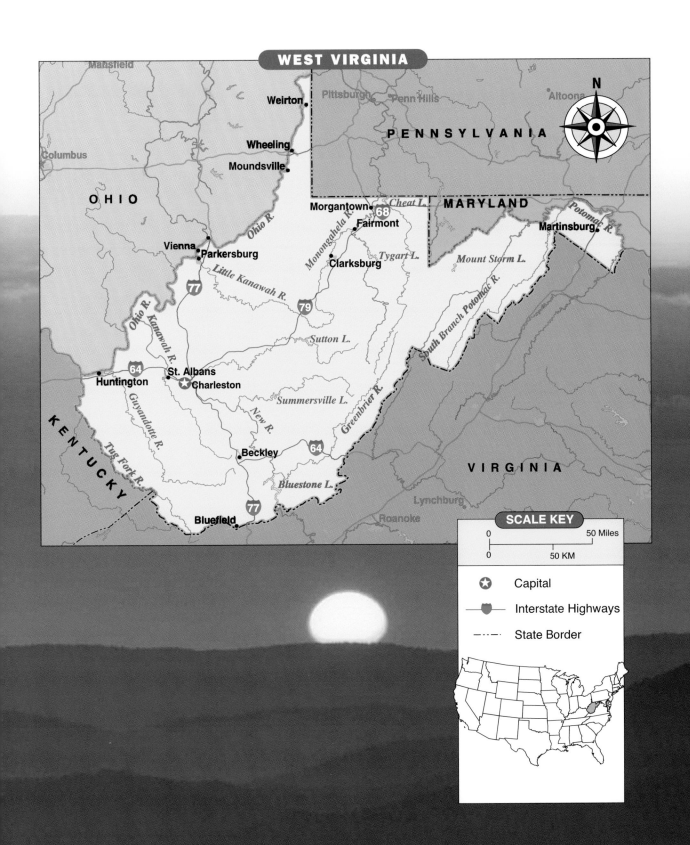

WEST VIRGINIA

Mansfield

Weirton

Pittsburgh   Penn Hills   Altoona

N

PENNSYLVANIA

Wheeling

Columbus

Moundsville

OHIO

Ohio R.

Morgantown   *Cheat L.*   **MARYLAND**

Fairmont 68

Monongahela R.   *Potomac R.*

Martinsburg

Vienna   *Tygart L.*

Parkersburg   **Clarksburg**   *Mount Storm L.*

77   *Little Kanawah R.*

South Branch Potomac R.

79

Ohio R.

Sutton L.

Kanawah R.

64   **St. Albans**   *Summersville L.*   *Greenbrier R.*

Huntington   ⭐ **Charleston**

KENTUCKY   *Guyandotte R.*   *New R.*

VIRGINIA

64   **Beckley**

Bluestone L.   Lynchburg

Tug Fork R.   77   Roanoke

Bluefield

Fast Facts

WEST VIRGINIA (WV), The Mountain State, The Panhandle State

Entered Union

June 20, 1863 (35th state)

Capital . . . . **Population**

Charleston 53,421

Total Population (2000)

1,808,344 (37th most populous state) — *Between 1990 and 2000, the state's population increased 0.8 percent.*

Largest Cities . . . . **Population**

Charleston 53,421
Huntington 51,475
Parkersburg 33,099
Wheeling 31,419
Morgantown 26,809

Land Area

24,078 square miles (62,362 square kilometers) (41st largest state)

State Motto

Montani Semper Liberi — *Latin for "Mountaineers Are Always Free."*

State Songs

"The West Virginia Hills," *words by David King in 1879, music by H. E. Engle;* "This Is My West Virginia," *words and music by Ires Bell;* "West Virginia, My Home Sweet Home," *words and music by Julian G. Hearne, Jr.; all adopted in 1963.*

State Bird

Cardinal

State Fish

Brook trout

State Insect

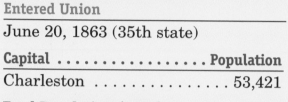

Honeybee

State Animal

Black bear — *Black bears climb trees easily and can sprint up to 35 miles per hour (56.3 kilometers per hour). Black bears do not always have black fur. Their fur can be chocolate brown, cinnamon brown, or blue-black. Black bears are smaller than brown bears and have shorter fur and claws.*

State Flower

Rhododendron — *These evergreen shrubs have large, round clusters of trumpet-shaped flowers. Rhododendrons bloom in a variety of colors from early spring to midsummer. They can grow up to 30 feet (9.1 m) tall.*

State Tree

Sugar maple

State Fruit

Golden Delicious apple

State Colors

Gold and blue

PLACES TO VISIT

Blackwater Falls State Park, *Davis*

The park offers hiking, horseback riding, nature programs, and other outdoor fun, plus a chance to see the 65-foot (19.8-m) Blackwater Falls. The falls are six stories high!

State Capitol Complex, *Charleston*

The spectacular gold-leaf rotunda is 5 feet (1.5 m) higher than the U.S. Capitol's dome. The rock crystal chandelier hanging from its center weighs 2 tons (1.8 metric tons). The complex also includes the governor's mansion, the Booker T. Washington Memorial, and the State Museum, which shows West Virginia's history from Native American days to the early twentieth century.

For other places and events, see p. 44.

BIGGEST, BEST, AND MOST

- The world's largest sycamore tree is on the Elk River in Webster Springs.

- The world's first and largest clothespin factory was located in Richwood.

- The telescope at the National Radio Astronomy Observatory in Green Bank is the largest fully movable radio telescope in the world.

STATE FIRSTS

- 1756 The nation's first public spa opened in Bath, Virginia, which is now Berkeley Springs, West Virginia.

- 1787 James Rumsey launched the first steamboat on the Potomac River.

- 1815 James Wilson accidentally discovered the nation's first natural gas source at Charleston.

- 1861 The first Union soldier killed by enemy action in the Civil War died on May 22 at Fetterman, near Grafton.

State of State Parks

More than 200,000 acres (80,940 hectares) of state parks, forests, and wildlife management lands are scattered throughout West Virginia. Forty-four state parks and forests offer some of the best fishing in the East and give visitors a chance to learn about nature. Seventeen of the state's parks offer weekly nature programs; eight have a naturalist on staff year-round.

The Steel-Drivin' Man

In the early 1870s, workers removed more than one mile (1.6 km) of rock to make a tunnel for the Chesapeake and Ohio Railroad. They broke every inch of it away by hand, using only steel picks, shovels, and the strength of their bodies. Although historical records are incomplete, John Henry is believed to have been one of those workers. Henry's claim to fame is the song that tells how the "steel-drivin' man" pitted his strength against the newly invented automated steam hammer — and won! John Henry dug farther than the machine. Exhausted but triumphant, he dropped down dead. Legend has it that at night, folks can still hear his hammer echoing through the mountains. As machines take over jobs formerly done by people, John Henry's legend becomes an important symbol of what people can do with their own two hands. The John Henry Monument in Talcott continues to inspire visitors.

Independent and Resourceful

> . . . he who would be no slave must consent
> to have no slave.
>
> — *Abraham Lincoln, in a letter dated April 6, 1859*

Three hundred million years ago, the land that is now West Virginia lay beneath an inland sea. This sea was home to coral, an animal that builds a tubular shell from minerals it derives from the water. Blue-gray, pink, and red chunks of fossilized coral now turn up in West Virginia fields and quarries. This fossil coral, called lithostrotionella, is the official state gem. Some chunks weigh up to 15 pounds (6.8 kilograms).

Coal beds were formed when large masses of peat moss decayed under pressure. Many other kinds of prehistoric plants also thrived in West Virginia. Fossils of a variety of plant species have been found. The world's oldest known seeds were found in Randolph County. The seeds date from the Devonian period, 345 million years ago.

Many millennia after the sea dried up, the mountains emerged. As far back as 12,000 years ago, Paleo-Indians hunted herds of mammoths, mastodons, and caribou in the Kanawha Valley. As the climate warmed, mammoths and mastodons died out, but deer were still plentiful and people settled in the area.

Early Days

Archaeological evidence indicates that the Adena, ancestors of modern Native Americans, flourished in this area for many years. Also called Mound Builders, they built hundreds of large dirt mounds along the Ohio and Kanawha Rivers. Their largest mounds were built as ceremonial sites. Smaller ones were the graves of their leaders, containing log tombs under piles of soil. Inside the mounds, archaeologists have uncovered elaborately adorned skeletons, pottery, and objects carved from soft stone.

Native Americans of West Virginia
Adena
Cherokee (Keetoowha)
Delaware
Mingo
Shawnee
Susquehanna
Tuscarora

DID YOU KNOW?

The great frontiersman Daniel Boone lived in West Virginia for about ten years. After he lost his land in Kentucky, Boone came to the Kanawha Valley. He hunted for beavers, otters, foxes, and raccoon with traps and his trusty tomahawk. In 1789, Daniel Boone was elected to the state government. In 1799, the restless adventurer moved on to Missouri.

The Adena were the first Native Americans to build such mounds. Older ceremonial graves, such as the Egyptian pyramids (2700 B.C.) have been found only in other countries. Soil tests on the largest conical burial mound in the United States tell scientists that the Adena built Moundsville's Grave Creek Mound sometime between 250 and 150 B.C. The Grave Creek Mound contains some 60,000 tons (54,420 metric tons) of soil. The mounds were built without any machinery, so archaeologists reason that a stable food supply allowed the Adena to devote many hours to efforts beyond basic survival. The first European to discover the Grave Creek Mound was a settler who tumbled off the top while hunting in 1770.

The Adena lived in permanent villages. The walls of their homes were made with poles lashed together or covered with woven straw. The roofs were also straw, or covered with mats. The Adena made knives and arrowheads from flint, a hard, gray stone. They also used other kinds of stone, as well as wood, bones, and antlers, to make tools.

They mixed crushed mussel shells into the clay for their pottery. The Adena created beautiful art, among the finest of all the northern Native American tribes. Copper bracelets from the Great Lakes, volcanic glass beads from the Rocky Mountains, and shells from the Gulf of Mexico were all found in West Virginia — proving that ancient trade routes existed

▼ One of the largest mounds left by the Adena is at Moundsville in West Virginia's northern panhandle. The Adena left behind hundreds of such ceremonial and burial mounds, which is why they are known as the Mound Builders.

across the entire expanse of North America. Around 1500, the Mound Builders abandoned their villages. What happened to them remains a mystery.

By the 1640s, the Cherokee (Keetoowha), Delaware, Shawnee, Tuscarora, and Mingo peoples were using the mound area for hunting. They also gathered salt from the brine pools of the Kanawha River valley. Brine is very salty water. After the water evaporated, the salt left behind was used to preserve and flavor meat.

First Europeans

In 1606, England's King James I granted the land that is now West Virginia to the London Company for the Virginia Colony. However, the remote territory remained unexplored until 1669, when the Virginia colony's governor, Sir William Berkeley, commissioned a German explorer and physician named John Lederer to investigate the area. Lederer reached the Blue Ridge Mountains that year and returned to the area in 1670.

▼ English surveyors explored West Virginia in the 1700s. They marked trees with arrows to establish boundaries.

In 1671, British explorers Thomas Batts and Robert Fallam reached the New River where it enters West Virginia and found deserted villages and cornfields, but no Native Americans. They established an English claim on the land. In 1726, Morgan ap Morgan, a Welsh immigrant, traveled south from Pennsylvania and built a cabin at Bunker Hill, near Martinsburg. The following year, a group of German pioneers established New Mecklenburg on the bank of the Potomac, in what is now Shepherdstown. As a teenager, George Washington visited the area as part of a survey team exploring the Allegheny Mountains for Lord Thomas Fairfax in 1748.

As more settlers moved into the area, war broke out between the French and Native Americans on one side and the British and their American colonists on the other. A failed raid on the French, led by George Washington, helped trigger this conflict. The French and Indian War raged on and off from 1754 to 1763, when the French finally surrendered.

Fearing that further settlement would spark more violence, England's King George III forbade settling west of the Allegheny Mountains. Despite this proclamation, by 1775, at least thirty thousand pioneers occupied the land between the Alleghenies and the Ohio River. Scottish, Irish, Welsh, and German pioneers made their way from Pennsylvania, settling in the eastern panhandle and then along the Ohio River at Wheeling (1769), Point Pleasant (1774), and Parkersburg (1785). Treaties were signed with the Native Americans, but settlement and violence continued until the Shawnee were finally defeated at Point Pleasant in 1774.

War and the Quest for Statehood

The British invaded the Virginia colony three times during the Revolutionary War (1775–1783). While the American colonists were fighting for their independence from England, the people of what is now West Virginia were asking the Second Continental Congress for independence from the

"Stonewall" Jackson

Thomas "Stonewall" Jackson earned his nickname in the Civil War when General Barnard Bee described how Jackson's brigade held "like a stone wall" while other Confederates fell back from the Northern attack at the First Battle of Bull Run in July 1861. Jackson was born in 1824 and received little formal education until his appointment to the United States Military Academy at West Point. He was a brilliant soldier but an extremely eccentric man.

Jackson hoped to cure his poor eyesight by dunking his head in cold water with his eyes open for as long as he could hold his breath. He kept no chairs in his study and would read for hours standing up. He also ate standing up because he believed it would straighten out his intestines, and to further relieve his indigestion, he often wrapped his waist with cold towels. Jackson was accidentally shot in the left arm by his own men after the battle of Chancellorsville in 1863. Although his arm was successfully amputated, Jackson died of pneumonia soon afterwards.

Virginia colony. Although their request for a separate government was denied, the reasons behind the request remained.

During the early 1800s, it became increasingly clear that while eastern Virginia shared the social and economic interests of the South, the western part of the state had more in common with the North and the West. Eastern Virginians tended to be rich Episcopalians, while the western residents tended to be poor Baptists, Methodists, and Presbyterians. The geography of western Virginia dictated small farms and trade on rivers, as opposed to sprawling plantations and sea trade in the east. There were bitter disputes over slavery, taxes, education, and other issues. The citizens of western Virginia thought that the wealthy plantation owners had too much power in the state's government. In 1810, western Virginians officially protested unfair representation in the state legislature. Meanwhile, the debate over slavery was tearing the country — and Virginia — in half.

On October 16, 1859, abolitionist John Brown led a raid on the federal arsenal at Harpers Ferry. Brown was convinced that the only way to end slavery was to incite a violent slave revolt. He hoped that the raid would provide his followers with weapons. Brown's raiders, five blacks and sixteen whites, managed to take the arsenal, but they were all captured or killed within a day by Robert E. Lee and a squad of eighty marines. Brown was hanged in Charleston on December 2. However, the cause of abolishing slavery was far from dead.

▼ In 1924, a West Virginia Democrat named John W. Davis ran for president against Calvin Coolidge. After he lost, Davis devoted himself to practicing law. Shortly before his death, Davis argued against school desegregation in the famous case of *Brown v. Board of Education*.

The Civil War

When Abraham Lincoln was elected president in 1860 on an antislavery platform, Southern states believed that their way of life was threatened. They formed a confederacy (group) of states determined to secede from (leave) the Union to form their own government. On April 12, 1861, Confederate troops fired on Fort Sumter, a federal army fort in South Carolina. The Civil War had begun!

On April 17, Virginians voted at a state convention in Richmond on whether to side with the Northern Union or the Southern Confederacy. The majority voted to join the Confederacy, but the delegates from northwestern Virginia protested and decided to create their own state. On June 11, the Wheeling Convention delegates declared the secession illegal. They reorganized the state government as the Restored Government of Virginia and appointed Francis H. Pierpont governor.

On October 24, 1861, the western counties of Virginia voted for the creation of a new state called Kanawha. One month later, delegates changed the name to West Virginia. A new constitution was drafted and voters approved it. On June 20, 1863, President Lincoln officially admitted West Virginia into the Union as the thirty-fifth state.

Many Civil War battles were fought in West Virginia. One eastern panhandle town was captured and recaptured fifty-six times as Union and Confederate forces took turns occupying it. About thirty thousand West Virginians served in the Union army, and about eight thousand fought for the South. When the bloody war was finally over, Virginia asked West Virginia to reunite, but the new state refused.

West Virginia was in terrible turmoil. The war had destroyed a great deal of property and left the state deeply in debt. Neighbor had killed neighbor, and bitter feelings lingered. West Virginia's Confederate veterans were denied the right to vote until 1871. When West Virginia first became a state in 1863, the Union sympathizers who had pushed for statehood chose the northern panhandle city of Wheeling for the capital. In 1870, five years after the end of the Civil War, Confederate sympathizers who had regained political control changed the capital to Charleston. From 1875 to 1885, Wheeling was once again the state capital, until Charleston was finally fixed as the capital by a public vote.

Railroads and Recovery

After the Civil War, West Virginia had to rebuild, and the rich deposits of coal under a large part of the state provided both income and jobs. The creation of a network of railroads between 1880 and 1910 helped the state exploit this valuable resource. Manufacturing and mining towns sprang up at key sites along the tracks.

▲ The National Radio Astronomy Observatory opened in Green Bank in 1959. It is part of a network of observatories that uses radio waves to observe and record astronomical data — and to seek signs of intelligent life beyond our planet.

DID YOU KNOW?

Peter Tarr built the first iron furnace west of the Allegheny Mountains in West Virginia. His furnace and iron works supplied cannon balls to Commodore Oliver Hazard Perry during the Battle of Lake Erie in the War of 1812.

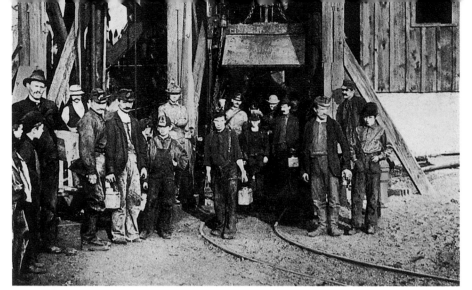

◄ Coal miners emerge from a mineshaft after spending nine hours toiling underground.

Mine owners took advantage of miners in need of work with shifts as long as eleven hours, minimal or nonexistent safety precautions, and low pay. A wage of fifty to seventy cents per day was not uncommon. Miners were often forced to live in company-owned towns where they had to pay huge amounts of money to rent their company-owned housing and buy basics like food and clothing at the company store. Many miners sickened and died from black lung disease, which was caused by breathing coal dust. Although the United Mine Workers of America sent union organizers into West Virginia in 1890, mine owners used all their power and riches to suppress the workers' attempts to form unions. In 1907, 361 miners died at Monongah in the nation's worst mine disaster.

In 1912, the United Mine Workers held its first strike. The state militia was called in, and twelve miners and nine mine guards were killed in the Mine Wars. The following year, newly elected Governor Henry D. Hatfield settled the strike by acting as a third-party negotiator.

World War I, in which the United States fought from 1917 to 1918, gave West Virginia a boost. The state profited from providing raw materials and manufactured goods for the war effort. By 1920, however, the coal mines were in trouble again. Five hundred federal soldiers were sent to quell rioting miners. The governor declared martial law, and the armed conflict lasted for a year. More than five hundred miners were arrested.

World War II (1941–1945) brought the state another boom time. West Virginia's chemical, glass, metal, and synthetic textile industries grew.

Henry Hatfield

Henry D. Hatfield was elected governor of West Virginia in 1912. His administration saw the creation of a Department of Public Health and one of the first workers' compensation laws in the nation. Hatfield also established a state Bureau of Labor and a state Road Bureau, promoted election reform, and improved the mine safety program. From 1929 to 1935, he served in the U.S. Senate.

Recent Times

West Virginia largely stays on the course dictated by its geography. Coal remains a major industry, although there may always be tension between the mine owners and the miners. In 1968, an explosion and fire at a coal mine in Farmington, which killed seventy-eight miners, led to the creation of stricter safety laws.

Floods periodically sweep through West Virginia's many valleys. In 1972, a coal waste dam on Buffalo Creek broke, and the resulting flood killed 118 people near Man. This disaster led to the Surface Mining Control and Reclamation Act of 1977, which requires that land disturbed for mining be restored to productive use, such as cropland, wetlands, and recreational areas.

Tourists from all over the nation travel to West Virginia for a wonderful vacation site rich in history, culture, crafts, and natural beauty. The state's diversified economy also makes full use of other natural resources, including timber, natural gas, petroleum, salt, and building stone.

Famous Feud

West Virginia was one of the sites of the most famous feud in U.S. history. The bloody dispute between the Hatfield family of West Virginia and the McCoys of Kentucky raged for nearly three decades, from 1863 to 1891. The story rivals anything Hollywood screenwriters could invent. The feud began with the murder of Asa Harmon McCoy, who defied his largely Confederate family by joining the Union army. The strongly Confederate Hatfields committed the crime, but the feud did not really heat up until years later with the theft of a pig, the murder of a witness, and the Romeo-and-Juliet romance between a young Hatfield and a young McCoy. The Hatfield and McCoy feud illustrates the lawless, isolated quality of that particular time and place — men from huge families enjoyed fighting and prided themselves on their marksmanship; police protection to stop the violence did not exist. Descendants of both families rose above their backgrounds to become governors, educators, and physicians.

Left: Captain William Anderson Hatfield (*seated, left*), leader of the Hatfield clan, had nine sons and loved playing pranks and telling tall tales.

Nice Neighbors

> Is it any wonder then,
> That my heart with rapture thrills
> As I stand once more with loved ones
> On those West Virginia Hills?
> . . . If o'er sea or land I roam,
> Still I'll think of happy home,
> And my friends among the West Virginia Hills.
> — *"The West Virginia Hills," by David King, 1879*

West Virginians are known as Mountaineers. They take much pride in their independence and freedom. The people who moved to West Virginia in the state's early days were often poor, but usually as rugged as the state's terrain. They were glad for a chance to farm in the state's fertile soil and grateful for its many deer and other wild game. Members of one family frequently remain in one town for many generations. Clan reunions are popular events throughout the state. Unlike most of the nation, West Virginia's population is largely rural; only about 36 percent of the population lives in cities. Vermont is the only state more rural than West Virginia.

Age Distribution in West Virginia
(2000 Census)

0–4	101,805
5–19	352,910
20–24	120,109
25–44	501,343
45–64	455,282
65 & over	276,895

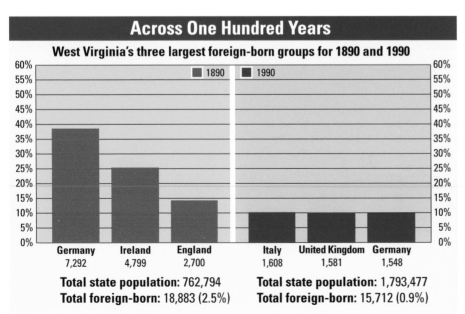

Across One Hundred Years

West Virginia's three largest foreign-born groups for 1890 and 1990

■ 1890 ■ 1990

| Germany 7,292 | Ireland 4,799 | England 2,700 | Italy 1,608 | United Kingdom 1,581 | Germany 1,548 |

Total state population: 762,794
Total foreign-born: 18,883 (2.5%)

Total state population: 1,793,477
Total foreign-born: 15,712 (0.9%)

Patterns of Immigration

The total number of people who immigrated to West Virginia in 1998 was 375. Of that number, the largest immigrant groups were from India (17.3%), Canada (7.2%), and China (6.1%).

Mountaineers know their neighbors and usually like them, although probably the most famous feud in American history took place between the Hatfields of West Virginia and the McCoys of Kentucky. Some West Virginians might object to the state's "hillbilly" image, but most Mountaineers believe there's nothing wrong with being a hillbilly — as long as the hills you call home are in West Virginia.

Ethnicities

Most of the area's first overseas settlers came from England, Scotland, Ireland, Wales, and Germany. Scottish immigrants compared Appalachia to their homeland. The state's growing mining, railroad, and lumber industries drew a wave of immigrants to West Virginia after the Civil War. Many of these new workers came from Hungary, Italy, Poland, and Russia. African Americans from the deep South also moved north to work in West Virginia.

Few foreign immigrants have come to the state since the beginning of the twentieth century. In fact, almost all of today's Mountaineers were born in the United States.

Diversity vs. Stereotypes

Outsiders often stereotype West Virginians as hillbillies who are constantly feuding with their neighbors. But the state is home to a variety of people, including Asians, African Americans, and many other ethnic groups. In 1996 and 2002, the Rockefeller Foundation for the Humanities awarded the

▲ Clarksburg's Italian Heritage Festival includes singers, dancers, and puppeteers.

DID YOU KNOW?

▌In the 1950s, when mechanization caused many West Virginia miners to lose their jobs, they moved to Michigan and Ohio. In the mid-1980s, when the coal industry suffered a slump, many West Virginians moved to North Carolina.

Heritage and Background, West Virginia — Year 2000

▶ Here is a look at the racial backgrounds of West Virginians today. West Virginia ranks thirty-eighth among all U.S. states with regard to African Americans as a percentage of the population.

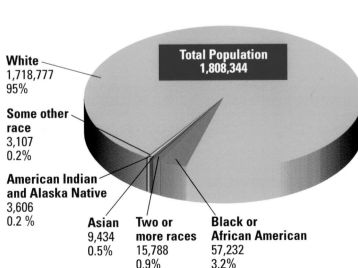

Total Population 1,808,344

White
1,718,777
95%

Some other race
3,107
0.2%

American Indian and Alaska Native
3,606
0.2 %

Native Hawaiian and Other Pacific Islander
400
0.02%

Asian
9,434
0.5%

Two or more races
15,788
0.9%

Black or African American
57,232
3.2%

Note: 0.7% (12,279) of the population identify themselves as **Hispanic** or **Latino,** a cultural designation that crosses racial lines. Hispanics and Latinos are counted in this category as well as the racial category of their choice.

Center for the Study of Ethnicity and Gender in Appalachia (CSEGA) scholars-in-residence grants to study the rich diversity of people in the state's isolated mountain communities. Scholars from across the United States have gathered at Marshall University in Huntington to conduct interviews with the many different people living in the Appalachians. Marshall's Art Department recently presented an exhibit called "Pointing the Way" to show how various ethnic groups have contributed to Appalachian culture.

West Virginians are a valuable resource for scholars seeking to learn about America's rich, rural past. The state's people are strong, resourceful, and hardworking. Many of the residents possess a great capacity for creativity, which is especially evident in the scope and skill of their arts, crafts, and soulful music.

Educational Levels of West Virginia Workers (age 25 and over)	
Less than 9th grade	123,622
9th to 12th grade, no diploma	182,192
High school graduate, including equivalency	486,334
Some college, no degree or associate degree	258,473
Bachelor's degree	109,651
Graduate or professional degree	73,309

▼ The skyline of Charleston, West Virginia's capital and largest city.

Religion

More than 80 percent of West Virginia's population practices some form of Christianity. The largest denomination (church or religious group) is Baptists, followed by Methodists, Roman Catholics, Presbyterians, Episcopalians, Disciples of Christ, Lutherans, Amish, Mennonites, and Church of the Brethren.

West Virginians of English ancestry tend to belong to Baptist or Episcopalian congregations. Those of Scotch-Irish descent are usually Presbyterians. West Virginia's eastern panhandle is home to many people with German backgrounds of the Amish, Mennonite, or Church of the Brethren congregations. The state's Roman Catholics tend to be eastern and southern Europeans concentrated near the state's industrial centers and coalfields.

Education

Schools form the proud heart of many West Virginia communities. In pioneer days, log cabin schools doubled as churches. Today, many rural schools are being consolidated to create larger schools that can offer better equipment, but Mountaineers fear that small communities may lose focus without their schools.

West Virginia's free school system was established soon after the state joined the Union in 1863. Before then, schools were mostly private and often religious. Young Mountaineers are required to attend school from age six to sixteen.

Marshall University and West Liberty State College in West Liberty, the state's first institutions of higher learning, opened in 1837. The state's largest university is West Virginia University in Morgantown, which opened in 1867, two years after the end of the Civil War. West Virginia State College opened in the city of Institute in 1891. The state has several other colleges scattered throughout. The first president of the Republic of Nigeria, Nnamdi Azikiwe, attended Storer College in Harpers Ferry. Storer College was founded in 1867 as one of the first U.S. colleges to educate former slaves.

Appalachian Aid

When John F. Kennedy campaigned for the presidency in West Virginia, he drew attention to the problems of Appalachia, a region including parts of West Virginia and eleven other states. Kennedy promised to help the Appalachians with their worst problems: unemployment, population loss, and industrial shutdowns. The Appalachian Regional Development Act provided $1.1 billion to build highways to stimulate commerce, industry, and tourism, and for health centers, job training, and other social programs.

Mountains and Valleys

The valleys between West Virginia's mountains are so narrow the dogs have to wag their tails up and down, instead of sideways.

— *A local joke*

A glance at the map reveals how West Virginia earned its nicknames, the Mountain State and the Panhandle State. Hardly any of its 24,230 square miles (62,755 sq km) of total area are flat! The only landlocked South Atlantic state, West Virginia lies entirely within the Appalachian Mountains. With an average elevation of 1,500 feet (457 m), West Virginia is the highest state east of the Mississippi River. The state has two panhandles: one in the north, which pokes between Pennsylvania and Ohio, and one in the northeast, between Maryland and Virginia. West Virginia's boundaries wiggle and squiggle along rivers and mountain ridges, touching on Pennsylvania and Ohio in the north, Maryland in the northeast, Virginia in the east and south, and Ohio and Kentucky in the west.

Valley and Plateau

Folded sedimentary rocks lie beneath all of West Virginia, which explains why its topography ranges from hilly to mountainous. In the east, the rock is more strongly folded,

Highest Point
Spruce Knob
4,861 feet (1,481 m)
above sea level

▼ *From left to right:*
Glade Creek Grist Mill; a sugar maple tree in autumn; a black bear; mist covered mountains; Blackwater Falls; Highland Scenic Highway.

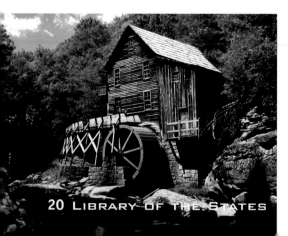

producing the narrow ridges and steep valleys of what is known as the Valley and Ridge Region. Caves are common in this area of forested mountains and fast-flowing streams.

To the west rises the state's biggest region, the Allegheny Plateau, which covers three-fifths of West Virginia. The highest elevations in the Mountain State are found along the eastern edge of the plateau, at Spruce Knob, which is 4,862 feet (1,481 m) above sea level, and Big Spruce Knob, which is 4,652 feet (1,418 m) above sea level.

West Virginia's steep slopes and shallow, clay, acidic soil favor forest growth over farms. Patches of more fertile soil can be found in the floodplains of rivers and where limestone bedrock neutralizes the acidity.

Climate

Large differences in altitude cause considerable variation in both temperature and rainfall within the Mountain State. Overall, West Virginia has a humid continental climate, with warm summers and cool to cold winters. The coldest temperatures and heaviest rainfall occur on the eastern edge of the Allegheny Plateau, where elevations are highest. Thick fog and several feet of snow often cover West Virginia's mountain peaks, while the valleys tend to be hot and humid.

Rain is plentiful in West Virginia. Because of the steep, narrow valleys, flash flooding is the state's most feared weather-related phenomenon. On the average, a major flood occurs in West Virginia every eighteen months. Summer thunderstorms often account for flash floods. Tornadoes and hurricanes rarely cause damage to the Mountain State.

Rivers and Lakes

The Monongahela and Kanawha River systems drain most of West Virginia into the Ohio River, which flows along the state's northwestern border. The Potomac River marks the

Average January temperature
Huntington:
 34.5°F (1.4°C)
Elkins: 30°F (-1.1°C)

Average July temperature
Huntington:
 75.5°F (24.2°C)
Elkins: 68.5°F (20.3°C)

Average yearly rainfall
Huntington:
 39 inches (99.1 cm)
Elkins: 43 inches
 (109.2 cm)

Average yearly snowfall
Huntington:
 23 inches (58.4 cm)
Elkins:
 67 inches (170.2 cm)

Largest Lakes

Bluestone Lake
6,011 acres
(2,433 ha)

Stonewall Jackson Lake
3398 acres
(1,375 ha)

Sutton Lake
3,391 acres
(1,372 ha)

Tygart Lake
2982 acres
(1,207 ha)

Summersville Lake
2,647 acres
(1,071 ha)

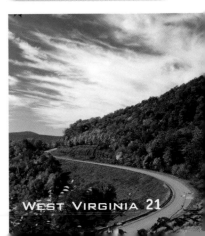

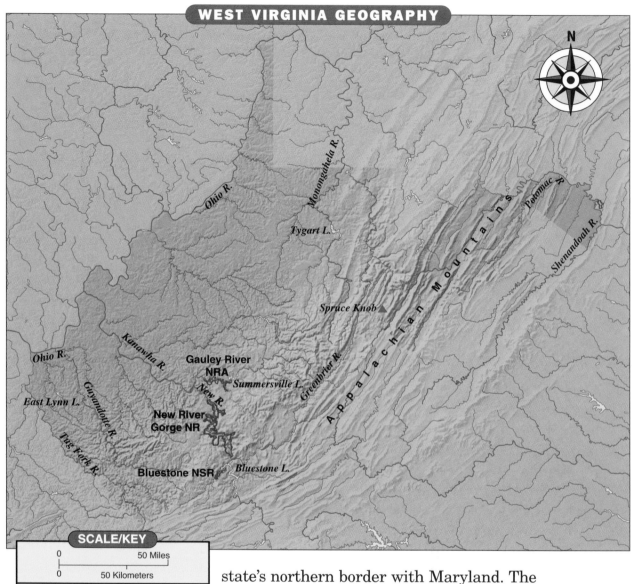

Ohio R.

Monongahela R.

Tygart L.

Potomac R.

Shenandoah R.

Spruce Knob ▲

Kanawha R.

Gauley River NRA

Ohio R.

New R.

Summersville L.

Greenbrier R.

Appalachian Mountains

East Lynn L.

Guyandotte R.

New River Gorge NR

Tug Fork R.

Bluestone NSR

Bluestone L.

SCALE/KEY

0	50 Miles
0	50 Kilometers

NR	National River
NRA	National Recreation Area
NSR	National Scenic River
▲	Highest Point
▨	Mountains

state's northern border with Maryland. The Shenandoah River drains the northeastern part of the state, along with other tributaries of the Potomac. Many other rivers also cross the Mountain State, which is famous with canoeists and kayakers for its whitewater adventures.

West Virginia has no large, natural lakes, but several big lakes were created by damming rivers. These lakes include Bluestone, Summersville, East Lynn, and Tygart.

Plants and Animals

About three-quarters of West Virginia is woodlands. The most common trees are basswood, beech, buckeye, cherry, hemlock, hickory, maple, oak, pine, spruce, and tulip trees. Many flowering plants thrive on West Virginia's plentiful rain and sunshine, including asters, azaleas, dogwoods, goldenrod, laurels, redbuds, and rhododendrons. Black-eyed Susans, red poppies, purple clover, white daisies, and crab apples grow wild all over the state.

Beavers, black bears, bobcats, gray foxes, groundhogs, mink, opossums, otters, rabbit, raccoon, red foxes, skunks, squirrels, and white-tailed deer are among the animals that roam the Mountain State. Brown thrashers, cardinals, ducks, eagles, falcons, geese, grebes, hawks, loons, quail, scarlet tanagers, snipes, sparrows, woodpeckers, and wood thrushes are just some of the state's birds. Game birds include ruffled grouse and wild turkeys. West Virginia's rushing rivers, streams, lakes, and ponds are home to a variety of fish: bass, bluegill, crappie, muskellunge, perch, pickerel, trout, walleyed pike, and more. Twenty species of snake live in West Virginia. Two of the most dangerous are the timber rattlesnake and the copperhead. American peregrine falcons, bald eagles, Cheat Mountain salamanders, Virginia big-eared bats, and Virginia northern flying squirrels are among the endangered and threatened animals that find shelter in the Mountain State.

Major Rivers

Guyandotte River
166 miles (267 km)

Ohio River
981 miles (1,579 km)

Potomac River
383 miles (616 km)

Kanawha River
352 miles (566 km)

▼ The New River, despite its name, has been flowing in its current location longer any other U.S. river and was first visited by Native Americans in prehistoric times. Famous for its rapids, the New River flows past Hinton.

Coal and Kayaks

> A West Virginia farmer farmed a hillside so steep
> he kept falling out of his cornfield. His neighbor
> had an orchard that went straight up a mountain.
> At harvest time he could shake the trees and the
> apples rolled right down into the cellar.
>
> — *A local joke about West Virginia's steep farmland*

West Virginia has a history of high unemployment
and poverty. As farmers put it, the state has had
a hard row to hoe. The Civil War plunged the state
into debt, but two other wars helped West Virginia recover
and develop its industries. The state supplied vast amounts
of coal and other necessary raw materials and chemicals
during World Wars I and II. West Virginia's prosperity has
risen and fallen with that of its great natural resource, coal.
Now the state is trying to further diversify its economy by
expanding industry and tourism and improving education
and health services. The state raises funds with a six percent
sales tax on consumer goods.

Agriculture and Forestry

West Virginia's rugged land is not well suited to large-scale
farming. The average size of West Virginia's approximately
twenty thousand farms is only 176 acres (71 ha). Since World
War II, many farmers have switched from general farming
to livestock breeding to take advantage of the state's bountiful
crop of hay.

Beef cattle, hay, chickens, milk, turkeys, apples, corn,
hogs, and tobacco are West Virginia's leading farm products.
The state also produces significant crops of oats, wheat,
beans, beets, cabbage, peaches, cherries, and blackberries.

Lumber has been a major source of income for West
Virginia, because three-quarters of the state is covered with
forest. Forests were harvested for fuel during the nineteenth
century and for lumber during the twentieth century to build

Top Employers
(of workers age sixteen and over)
Services 42.7%
Wholesale and retail trade 15.9%
Manufacturing . . .11.9%
Transportation, communications, and public utilities 8.2%
Construction 7.0%
Finance, insurance, and real estate . . 4.6%
Federal, state, and local government (including military) 5.8%
Agriculture, forestry, fisheries, and mining 4.1%

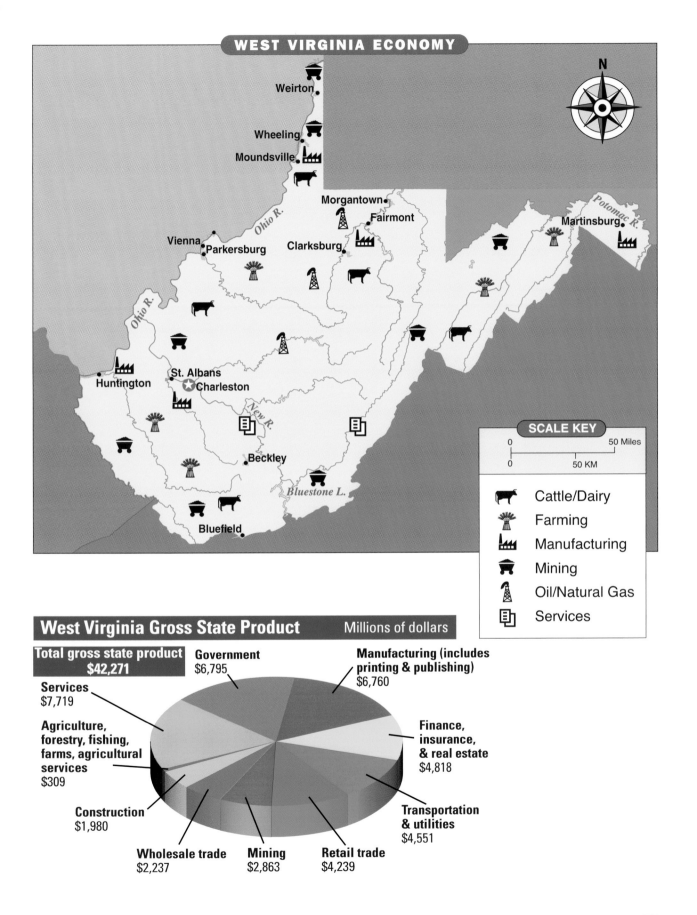

WEST VIRGINIA ECONOMY

Weirton

Wheeling
Moundsville

Morgantown
Fairmont

Martinsburg

Vienna
Parkersburg

Clarksburg

Ohio R.

Potomac R.

Ohio R.

Huntington

St. Albans
Charleston

New R.

Beckley

Bluestone L.

Bluefield

SCALE KEY

| 0 | | 50 Miles |
| 0 | 50 KM | |

🐂 Cattle/Dairy

🌾 Farming

🏭 Manufacturing

⛏ Mining

🛢 Oil/Natural Gas

📑 Services

West Virginia Gross State Product — Millions of dollars

Total gross state product $42,271

Government $6,795

Manufacturing (includes printing & publishing) $6,760

Services $7,719

Finance, insurance, & real estate $4,818

Agriculture, forestry, fishing, farms, agricultural services $309

Transportation & utilities $4,551

Construction $1,980

Wholesale trade $2,237

Mining $2,863

Retail trade $4,239

Coal is vital to West Virginia's economy, but automation has reduced the number of jobs for miners.

towns throughout the eastern United States. In the 1920s and 1930s, forest fires and erosion, which contributed to flooding, made it clear that such rapid exploitation could not continue. Large national and state forests were established, and many of the areas that were once harvested have grown back.

Mining

West Virginia's most famous industry is the mining of bituminous coal. (Bitumen is a tarlike substance used for road surfaces and roofs.) Since the early twentieth century, the state has consistently been among the nation's top two or three states in annual coal production. West Virginia has an estimated four percent of the world's coal supply.

Coal was first found in West Virginia in 1742 near Racine, but large-scale industry did not develop until after the Civil War. Then out-of-state investors opened coal mines, drilled petroleum and gas wells, and built railroads and factories.

Coal production peaked in 1918 during World War I and in 1947 just after World War II. In 1988, Wyoming became the nation's overall leading coal producer. However, coal continues to be key to West Virginia's economy. When the entire coal industry slumped in the mid-1980s, West Virginia measured in with the nation's highest unemployment rate — 18 percent. Scientists estimate that 40 percent of West Virginia has mineable coal and that a large percentage of the state's coal has yet to be mined.

Natural gas and petroleum add to the state's mineral wealth. West Virginia's petroleum boom began in 1860 with the drilling of a successful well at Burning Springs. Other major mineral products include limestone, sand and gravel, salt, and clay. West Virginia usually ranks among the nation's top ten states in the annual value of its mineral output.

Manufacturing

West Virginia's natural resources are the basis for most of its manufacturing industries: primary and fabricated metals,

Parks and Tourism

Although the Great Depression of the 1930s affected the entire country, West Virginia was hit harder than most other states. Thousands of miners lost their jobs. Franklin D. Roosevelt's New Deal created government jobs through the Works Progress Administration (WPA) from 1935–1943, which included clearing paths for hiking. Many of these paths are part of the state's growing tourism industry today. West Virginia now maintains forty-four state parks and forests. Like many states with a wealth of natural beauty, West Virginia hopes to strengthen its economy against future slumps by providing tourists from all over the United States and the world with a perfect vacation destination. The parks also offer educational and historical programs.

glass, chemicals, wood products, printed materials, textiles and apparel, processed food, electronic equipment, and machinery. Dye, paint, rubber, plastic, and soap are also produced in West Virginia. In 1943, the first synthetic rubber plant opened near Charleston.

Thanks to plentiful supplies of fine silica sand and natural gas to fuel furnaces, the glass industry is important in West Virginia. When silica sand is heated enough to melt, it forms molten glass. Some of the state's factories make plate glass, tubing, and building blocks, but others use centuries-old techniques to produce masterpieces of handblown glass. Clay deposits along the Ohio River have contributed to West Virginia's pottery industry.

▲ West Virginia's eastern panhandle grows apples and peaches. The state ranks ninth nationwide in the production of apples. The Golden Delicious variety was first grown in West Virginia.

Transportation, Services, and Tourism

Rugged terrain has slowed but not stopped the building of transportation facilities in West Virginia. About 35,000 miles (56,315 km) of roads cross the state, including some 555 miles (893 km) of interstate highways. About 2,800 miles (4,023 km) of railroad tracks carry coal and other primary products throughout West Virginia. Coal and other bulky products are also shipped by truck and by river. A pipeline network transports petroleum and gas.

West Virginia has approximately sixty airports and twenty-three heliports. Charleston's Yeager Airport — named in honor of test pilot Chuck Yeager — is the busiest.

West Virginia generates its own electricity, mostly from coal-fired plants. The state produces enough electricity to export power to other states.

Tourism is one of West Virginia's biggest industries, providing about fifty thousand jobs. While commercial fishing is not significant to West Virginia's economy, fishing and hunting are major recreational industries.

Made in West Virginia

Leading farm products and crops
Beef cattle
Chickens
Turkeys
Apples
Corn
Hay
Milk
Tobacco

Other products
Automotive parts
Coal
Machinery
Natural gas

Major Airports		
Airport	Location	Passengers per year (2000)
Yeager Airport	Charleston	545,962
Tri-State Airport	Huntington	110,794
Wood County Airport	Parkersburg	47,204

Democrats Since the Depression

> These unhappy times call for the building of plans . . . that build from the bottom up and not from the top down, that put their faith once more in the forgotten man at the bottom of the economic pyramid.
>
> — *President Franklin Delano Roosevelt in a radio address, April 7, 1932*

West Virginia was formed by politics, when the western counties of Virginia refused to leave the Union with the rest of their state during the Civil War. The state's first constitution was adopted in its first year of statehood, 1863, but the current government is based on a second constitution, adopted nine years later in 1872. Like the federal government, West Virginia's government is divided into three branches to maintain a balance of power.

The Executive Branch

The governor is the head of the executive branch. The governor may serve any number of four-year terms, but no more than two in a row. The other members of the executive branch include the secretary of state, the attorney general, the auditor, the treasurer, and the commissioner of agriculture. All serve four-year terms.

West Virginia has no lieutenant governor. If the governor cannot complete his or her term, the president of the state senate takes over until the next election.

The Legislative Branch

West Virginia's legislature includes a thirty-four-member senate and a one-hundred-member house of delegates. Senators are elected by popular vote to four-year terms. Delegates are elected to two-year terms.

The legislature votes on whether to add new laws to West Virginia's government and whether to make changes to existing laws. Proposed new laws — called bills — are submitted to the

State Constitution

"The state of West Virginia is, and shall remain, one of the United States of America. The Constitution of the United States of America, and the laws and treaties made in pursuance thereof, shall be the supreme law of the land.

— Preamble to the West Virginia State Constitution 1863

Elected Posts in the Executive Branch		
Office	Length of Term	Term Limits
Governor	4 years	2 consecutive terms
Secretary of State	4 years	none
Attorney General	4 years	none
Commissioner of Agriculture	4 years	none
Auditor	4 years	none
Treasurer	4 years	none

DID YOU KNOW?

The youngest person ever elected by popular vote to the U.S. Senate was born in Weston. Rush D. Holt was twenty-nine when elected in 1934. Holt had to wait until his thirtieth birthday in June 1935 to take his Senate seat.

governor, who may sign them into law or veto (reject) them.

The legislature may also propose changes to the state's constitution, but to take effect, such changes must win a majority of votes in a general election. Changes to the state constitution may also be proposed by holding a constitutional convention.

The Judicial Branch

This branch of the government contains three levels of judges and courts. The state supreme court of appeals is the highest. Its five justices are elected to twelve-year terms. The chief justice is the member who has served the longest. The supreme court hears appeals from the lower courts. It also protects the state's constitution by determining whether the other two branches of government have disobeyed the state's laws.

The circuit courts decide major trials, involving crimes with long sentences (jail terms). The circuit courts are served by a total of sixty judges elected to eight-year terms.

In cases of civil law, which deal with private matters that are neither criminal nor political, magistrate courts settle disputes that involve $3,000 or less. Municipal courts rule on minor offenses, like traffic violations. Family courts deal with matters such as divorce, child support, and adoption.

▼ The gold dome of the state capitol shines in Charleston's historic East End.

Local Government

West Virginia is divided into fifty-five counties, each of which elects a three-member county court. The people of each county also vote for the county clerk, sheriff, and prosecuting attorney.

In addition, West Virginia has 161 cities and towns. Those cities with populations of more than two thousand may adopt their own charters (list of rights and rules), as long as they do not conflict with state laws.

National Representation

Like every other state in the Union, West Virginia holds two seats in the U.S. Senate in Washington, D.C. The state also elects three Representatives to serve in the U.S. House of Representatives. States with larger populations are allowed to have more Representatives.

West Virginia has five electoral votes, which help decide the outcome of presidential elections. States with larger populations also have more electoral votes.

West Virginia Politics

The Union sympathizers who pushed for West Virginia to become a separate state from Virginia were mostly supporters of the first Republican president, Abraham Lincoln. The state stayed largely Republican until the Great Depression of the 1930s. Many West Virginians were persuaded to switch to the Democratic party by Franklin Delano Roosevelt's promise of a "New Deal," which offered the nation's poor and jobless hope for the future.

Since 1932, few Republican presidential candidates have won in West Virginia. By the end of the 1990s, registered Democrats outnumbered Republicans in the state by more than two to one.

Government in Action

One function of West Virginia's government is to guarantee that all the state's citizens are treated fairly. To make sure

State Legislature			
House	Number of Members	Length of Term	Term Limits
Senate	34 senators	4 years	none
House of Delegates	100 delegates	2 years	none

that civil rights are being protected in the state, the West Virginia Advisory Committee to the U.S. Commission on Civil Rights has held community forums where citizens discuss problems like police brutality, hate crimes, violence in schools, and discrimination on the job. The Commission has made recommendations for ways the state can improve its treatment of people with disabilities, as well as minority ethnic and religious groups.

These recommendations include hiring and promoting more minority and female police officers, teachers, and school administrators. The state is also investigating ways to ensure that even small businesses do not discriminate against minorities in hiring. In 1992, the state formed the Hate Crime Task Force to advise the West Virginia Human Rights Commission and coordinate with police, civil rights groups, schools, and communities in finding better ways to prevent and respond to hate crimes.

Cecil H. Underwood

West Virginia's youngest governor was also its oldest! Cecil H. Underwood took office as governor in 1959 at the age of thirty-seven. He served two terms and then was elected again in 1996 at age seventy-four.

Below: Governor Cecil Underwood addresses nine hundred teenagers who came to Charleston on "Tobacco-Free Day" at the legislature in 1999. The governor asked the legislature for a first-ever tax on smokeless tobacco in West Virginia.

Hard Work and History

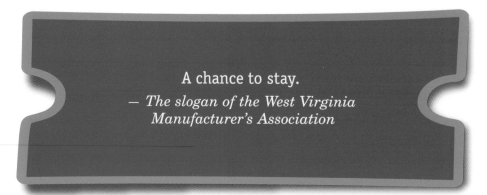

A chance to stay.

— *The slogan of the West Virginia
Manufacturer's Association*

West Virginia's history is scattered over the hilly ground from the Adena ceremonial mounds and the historic hot springs where George Washington soaked in an outdoor stone tub to the many Civil War battle sites and coal mines.

The prehistoric burial mound at Grave Creek Mound State Park in Moundsville is the largest of its kind: 69 feet (21 m) high and 900 feet (274 m) around the base. The mound was built by the Adena more than two thousand years ago. The nearby Delf Norona Museum and Cultural Center displays artifacts from Native American life in West Virginia from 1,000 B.C. to A.D. 1.

The Native Americans of the state considered the healing hot springs at Berkeley sacred. Tribal warfare was put aside to allow everyone a good soak. George Washington bathed in the springs in 1748, eight years before the springs were opened as a resort that people still enjoy today.

Prickett's Fort State Park in Fairmont is one of many places where visitors can learn about life in West Virginia in colonial times. The fort is a reconstruction of a 1774 original. Costumed guides and craftspeople show how West Virginians dressed, lived, and worked in the eighteenth century.

> **DID YOU KNOW?**
>
> **B**luegrass music derives from the Scotch-Irish traditional music of the southern Appalachian Mountains. It uses typical mountain dance-group instruments like mandolins, banjos, and fiddles.

▼ **The award-winning Greenbrier Valley Theatre in Lewisburg presents musicals, dramas, comedies, and children's plays year-round.**

The Harpers Ferry National Historical Park helps visitors understand what led to the Civil War. The 2,343-acre (948 ha) park has six Paths Through History: Industry, John Brown, Civil War, African-American History, Environmental History, and Transportation. Visitors can also see the Industry Museum, Wetlands Museum, John Brown's Fort, the Black Voices Museum, the Civil War Museum, and Jefferson Rock.

Independence Hall in Wheeling is the place where West Virginia decided its destiny. After Virginia left the Union in 1861, residents of the western counties met there to create the new state of West Virginia and its constitution. The building now houses a museum.

Jackson's Mill Historic Area in Weston is on the original 5-acre (2-ha) childhood home of the great Confederate general Thomas J. "Stonewall" Jackson. The site contains a community of eighteenth- and nineteenth-century buildings, including two furnished eighteenth-century log cabins. There are displays of blacksmithing and weaving equipment, carpentry tools, and other artifacts of life in West Virginia both before and after the Civil War.

Fifty acres (20 ha) of reconstructed buildings can be found at the West Virginia State Farm Museum in Point Pleasant. The museum has replicas of an old Lutheran

Tamarack

Tamarack: The Best of West Virginia is the nation's only statewide showcase of handicrafts, arts, furniture and woodcrafts, glassware, pottery, fiber arts (quilting, weaving, basket making), jewelry, painting, sculpture, music, books, and food. The 50,000-square-foot (4,650-square-meter) center north of Beckley features live crafts demonstrations, gallery exhibits, gardens, and a nature trail. Tamarack provides jobs, marketing, training, and education for artists, craftspeople, and farmers. The center also has a theater for live performances and films.

church, a one-room schoolhouse, print shop, doctor's office, country store, blacksmith shop, herb garden, railroad cars, farm equipment, and also features two log cabins built in the early 1800s.

The Beckley Exhibition Coal Mine in Beckley portrays how West Virginia's many miners worked and lived. A former mine serves as a living history exhibit. Visitors ride on remodeled mine cars and are guided by real coal miners. The tour includes a mine museum, a typical coal company house, and a trip through mine shafts.

Tourists learn about West Virginia's logging industry as they ride an old steam locomotive past mountain scenery to the top of one of the state's highest peaks, Bald Knob. Visitors experience the past in Cass, on the way to Bald Knob. In the early 1900s, Cass was a major lumber center. It is now one of America's best-preserved company towns.

Many glass factories and outlets offer tours that highlight glass-forming demonstrations. The State Museum at the Cultural Center in Charleston has a permanent exhibit about glassmaking, including a video that shows the process and history of the art.

▲ Visitors to the Exhibition Coal mine in Beckley are guided through the mine's underground chambers.

DID YOU KNOW?

The Mountain Heritage Arts and Crafts Festival at Harpers Ferry was honored by the Library of Congress among its "Local Legacies 2000." The fair, held in the spring and fall, features more than two hundred artisans demonstrating and selling their crafts, as well as bluegrass music and dance.

Libraries and Museums

West Virginia's cultural institutions are centered in Charleston, Wheeling, and Huntington, as well as in various college and university towns. The State Museum in Charleston and the Oglebay Institute Mansion Museum in Wheeling feature displays on the state's history. Charleston's Sunrise Foundation is a complex of buildings that includes an art gallery, museum, planetarium, and garden center. For displays as diverse as pre-Columbian art and local handicrafts, Georgian silver, and American and European paintings, visit the Huntington Museum of Arts in Huntington.

West Virginia has about 180 public libraries. The largest is in Charleston. Also in the state's capital is the West Virginia Division of Culture and History Library, with an extensive collection of records and documents concerning the state's history. The biggest academic library is in Morgantown, at West Virginia University.

Communications

West Virginia's first newspaper was the *Potomak Guardian & Berkeley Advertiser,* which was published in Shepherdstown in 1790. The state now has some twelve

DID YOU KNOW?

The Old Opera House Theatre in Charles Town was built in 1910. Now fully restored, the theater is on the National Historic Register.

▼ The country store at the Heritage Farm and Museum near Huntington is just one of many exhibits that depict Appalachian life from the 1850s through the 1950s.

West Virginia Public Radio's
MOUNTAIN STAGE

▶ West Virginia's public radio station presents a weekly variety show of live music that is broadcast from Charleston internationally via satellite.

daily newspapers. The most important ones are the *Charleston Daily Mail*, the *Charleston Gazette*, Huntington's *Herald-Dispatch*, and Wheeling's *News-Register*.

West Virginia has seven AM and forty-six FM radio stations and about seventeen television stations. The first radio station started broadcasting in 1923. The first television station, WSAZ-TV, began airing shows in 1949.

Music, Theater, and Crafts

Both bluegrass and country music have their roots in Appalachia. The state's oldest theater is the Capitol Music Hall, built in Wheeling in 1928. Since 1933, the music hall has hosted Jamboree USA, a celebration of country music. The theater has also presented Broadway plays and other top entertainment and is the home of Wheeling's symphony orchestra. Charleston also has its own symphony orchestra. Charleston and several other West Virginia cities have resident theater groups.

Fiddlers and mandolin players show up at almost every gathering in West Virginia. From early spring to late fall, the state is full of old-time, bluegrass, Cajun, and gospel music events. Mountaineers are also fond of playing the dulcimer, a traditional stringed instrument whose name comes from the Latin words for "sweet" and "song." Traditional clog dancing is still popular too.

Crafting beautiful things by hand is a tradition in West Virginia. Mountaineers enjoy many old-fashioned crafts like quilting, basket making, and pottery. Handicrafts are displayed at various fairs and galleries. The Augusta Heritage Center, now located at Davis and Elkins College, was started twenty-five years ago by a small group of people living in Elkins. Their idea was to revive interest in West Virginia crafts, dance, and music through workshops and other programs. Augusta was the name of the region during colonial times when many of the crafts taught there

> **DID YOU KNOW?**
>
> **C**arter Godwin Woodson, the man who pioneered the study of African-American history, was dean at West Virginia State College from 1920 to 1922. Though he was born in Virginia, Woodson attended Douglass High School in Huntington, and later was its principal for three years.

now were first practiced. Today, the center is a thriving gathering spot for artisans with interests in traditional folk arts, folklore, and music. In addition to supporting West Virginia crafts, Augusta's programs also promote an awareness of the handiwork of many ethnic cultures, such as African-American, French-Canadian, Cajun and Irish. Tourists and visitors from all fifty states and more than a dozen foreign countries have come to the Augusta Heritage Center to become involved in its programs.

Sports

Mountaineers work hard, and they also play hard. The beautiful, rugged landscape offers many opportunities to enjoy outdoor activities like fishing, hunting, skiing, horseback riding, bicycling, camping, mountain climbing, and golfing. Many of the state's urban residents head to the country for weekend fun and a chance to appreciate West Virginia's lovely landscapes and mountain vistas.

People who like canoeing, kayaking, and rafting appreciate the exciting challenge of running the rapids on West Virginia's Cheat and New Rivers. The state hosts many canoe and kayak meets, with downriver and slalom races. In 2001, the Gauley River hosted the World Rafting Championships. There are horse-racing tracks at Charles Town and Chester. Wheeling offers dog racing.

▶ George Brett of the Kansas City Royals kisses home plate at Kauffman Stadium after the last home game of his career. Brett got an eighth-inning hit that tied the game as the Royals went on to beat the Indians, 3–2.

Valiant West Virginians

> There is no greater calling than to serve your fellow man. There is no greater contribution than to help the weak. There is no greater satisfaction than to have done it well.
>
> — *Walter P. Reuther, president of the United Auto Workers union*

Following are a few of the thousands of people who were born, died, or spent much of their lives in West Virginia and made extraordinary contributions to the state and the nation.

JAMES RUMSEY
INVENTOR

BORN: *1743, Cecil County, MD*
DIED: *December 20, 1792, London, England*

Although James Rumsey did not receive much formal education, he was held in high esteem by men like George Washington and Ben Franklin for his ability as an inventor. On the Potomac at Shepherdstown on December 3,1787, Rumsey made a successful public demonstration of his design for a steamboat. The Rumseian Society, dedicated to publicizing and funding further development of the boat, sent him to England to raise funds and secure patents for his inventions. Rumsey died during that trip. A monument honoring Rumsey overlooks the Potomac, and a replica of his steamboat was built on the bicentennial of its demonstration in 1987. The inventor is remembered with a regatta each October in Shepherdstown.

FRANCIS H. PIERPONT
POLITICIAN AND GOVERNOR

BORN: *January 25, 1814, near Morgantown*
DIED: *March 24, 1899, Pittsburgh, PA*

Francis Pierpont provided leadership at the very beginning of West Virginia's history. He graduated from Allegheny College and later became the regional lawyer for the Baltimore and Ohio Railroad. As an active supporter of President Lincoln, Pierpont pulled together the loyal Unionists in the western part of Virginia when the state left the Union in 1861. In the same year, Pierpont was elected to command the government set up by the Wheeling Convention. In 1862, this new government gave approval, required by the U. S. Constitution, for the creation of an independent state now named West Virginia. From 1863 to 1865, Pierpont was governor of the Restored State of Virginia, and then from 1865 to 1868 governor of

Virginia. Known as a statesman, a statue of Pierpont is on display at the Capitol in the National Statuary Hall Collection. For his key role in the founding of the state, Pierpont became known as the Father of West Virginia.

THOMAS "STONEWALL" JACKSON
CONFEDERATE GENERAL

BORN: *January 21, 1824, Clarksburg*
DIED: *May 10, 1863, Chancellorsville, VA*

Orphaned at an early age, Thomas Jonathan Jackson graduated from West Point at twenty-two. He fought with distinction in the Mexican War (1846–1848), but resigned from the Army to teach at the Virginia Military Institute from 1851 to 1861. When the Civil War broke out, Jackson joined the Confederate Army. During the First Battle of Bull Run in 1861, he earned his famous nickname: Other Southern troops fell back, but Jackson's brigade stood "like a stone wall" against the Union Army. A brilliant tactician, Jackson contributed to many key Southern victories. Next to Robert E. Lee, he was the most important Confederate general. On May 2, 1863, Jackson was accidentally shot by some of his own men who mistook him for an enemy when he was returning to camp at night. He died eight days later.

BOOKER T. WASHINGTON
AFRICAN-AMERICAN LEADER

BORN: *April 5, 1856, Franklin County, VA*
DIED: *November 14, 1915, Tuskegee, AL*

Born to slaves in Franklin County, Virginia, Booker Taliaferro Washington moved to Malden with his family after the Civil War. As a child, Washington worked in coal mines for nine months of the year

and attended school for three. He worked his way through Hampton Institute, a school in Virginia established to educate former slaves. In 1881, he became the founder and first president of Tuskegee Institute, an Alabama trade school for African Americans. Under Washington's leadership, Tuskegee Institute became an important industrial and agricultural college that helped its students earn equality through education. Washington became a respected speaker and adviser on racial issues to Presidents Theodore Roosevelt and William Howard Taft. He wrote several books, including his acclaimed autobiography, *Up From Slavery.*

ANNA JARVIS
FOUNDER OF MOTHER'S DAY

BORN: *May 1, 1864, Webster*
DIED: *November 24, 1948, West Chester, PA*

Anna Jarvis was the ninth of eleven children born to Anna Maria and Granville Jarvis. Throughout her life, Jarvis was inspired by her mother, who had organized Mother's Day Work Clubs to improve health and sanitary conditions. In 1865, shortly after the end of the Civil War, and when Anna was only one year old, her mother held a Mother's Friendship Day, which brought together soldiers and neighbors of all political beliefs. At her mother's graveside in 1905, Anna swore to make her mother's wish come true. She wrote hundreds of letters to legislators and business leaders urging them to support the idea of honoring all mothers with a special day. In 1915, President Woodrow Wilson officially designated the second Sunday in May as the first nationally celebrated Mother's Day.

PEARL S. BUCK
AUTHOR

BORN: *June 26, 1892, Hillsboro*
DIED: *March 6, 1973, Danby, VT*

Although she was born in Hillsboro, Pearl Buck spoke Chinese before she learned English. The daughter of American missionaries, she lived in China until she was forty-one. She spent the second half of her life writing in West Virginia. China provided the setting for Buck's most popular books, including her 1932 Pulitzer prize-winning second novel, *The Good Earth*. Her twin biographies of her parents, *The Exile* and *Fighting Angel,* contributed to her becoming the third American to win the Nobel Prize for Literature in 1938. Buck also worked for humanitarian causes. During the 1960s, she founded Welcome House, an international, interracial adoption agency, and established the Pearl S. Buck Foundation, which helps improve the lives of children throughout the world.

WALTER P. REUTHER
UNION ORGANIZER

BORN: *September 1, 1907, Wheeling*
DIED: *May 9, 1970, Pellston, MI*

Walter Philip Reuther started working in a factory at sixteen and soon became involved in union work. He was prominent in the sit-down strikes of the late 1930s that helped establish the United Auto Workers (UAW). During his career, Reuther won many benefits for his union's members, including annual wage increases based on productivity, cost-of-living raises, and health and pension benefits. From 1946 until his death, Reuther was president of the UAW. He also led the Congress of Industrial Organizations (CIO) for three years, and helped arrange for its merger with the American Federation of Labor (AFL). Reuther served as vice president of the AFL-CIO from 1955 to 1968.

CYRUS R. VANCE
POLITICIAN AND DIPLOMAT

BORN: *March 27, 1917, Clarksburg*
DIED: *January 12, 2002, New York City*

A graduate of Yale Law School, Cyrus Roberts Vance began his government career as a special counsel for the Senate Armed Services Committee in 1957. He served as secretary of the Army from 1962 to 1964 and as deputy secretary of defense from 1964 to 1967. Vance took on several important diplomatic missions for President Lyndon Johnson, including settling a dispute between Greece and Turkey over Cyprus in 1967. During the Paris peace conference on Vietnam from 1968 to 1969, Vance was deputy chief of the U.S. delegation. As secretary of state under President Jimmy Carter, Vance was involved with the Strategic Arms Limitation Talks (SALT) and played a key role in discussions that resulted in the 1979 peace treaty between Israel and Egypt. He was also involved in the efforts to free U.S. hostages in Iran. In the 1990s, Vance was a United Nations mediator in the Balkan crisis.

CHUCK YEAGER
PILOT

BORN: *February 13, 1923, Myra*

Charles Elwood Yeager enlisted in the Army after high school. The young pilot shot down thirteen German planes during World War II. After the war, Yeager became a flight instructor and test pilot. In 1947, he became the first human being to travel faster than the speed of sound, 662 miles (1,066 km) per hour. In 1953, he set another world speed record: 1,650 miles (2,660 km) per hour. Yeager retired as a brigadier general in 1975. He wrote two autobiographies, *Yeager* and *Press On.* Yeager is a key figure in Tom Wolfe's 1979 book about the space program, *The Right Stuff,* which was made into a movie in 1983. Charleston's Yeager Airport was named in his honor.

DON KNOTTS
ACTOR

BORN: *July 21, 1924, Morgantown*

The son of farmers, Don Knotts started his show business career at thirteen as an amateur ventriloquist. He attended West Virginia University and served in the Army during World War II. Knotts met Andy Griffith when the two acted in *No Time for Sergeants* on Broadway. A 1958 film version of the play led to *The Andy Griffith Show,* in which Knotts created one of TV's most memorable characters. The role of Deputy Barney Fife won Knotts five supporting actor Emmys and a chance to perform in films like *The Incredible Mr. Limpet, The Shakiest Gun in the West,* and *The Apple Dumpling Gang.* Knotts continues to perform in films and television.

BETSY C. BYARS
CHILDREN'S BOOK AUTHOR

BORN: *August 7, 1928, Charlotte, NC*

Betsy Cromer Byars grew up in North Carolina. At college she majored in math until failing grades prompted a switch to English. In 1962, she moved to Morgantown and signed up for a children's literature course. In 1971, Byars's novel *Summer of the Swans* won the Newbery Medal. Byars has written more than fifty children's books translated into nineteen languages. She and her husband, both pilots, now live on an airstrip in South Carolina.

MARY LOU RETTON
OLYMPIC GYMNAST

BORN: *January 24, 1968, Fairmont*

Mary Lou Retton started gymnastics lessons at seven. At fourteen, she moved to Houston, Texas, to train with celebrated Romanian coach Bela Karolyi. At sixteen, Retton became the first American ever to win an individual all-around gold medal in gymnastics at the 1984 Olympics. She also won two silver medals (vault and team competition) and two bronze medals (floor exercise and uneven bars). Her stunning victory made her one of the most famous Olympic athletes in the world, a prized commercial representative, and the first female athlete to be pictured on the front of a Wheaties cereal box. Retton retired from competition in 1986 to become a motivational speaker. She is also involved with the President's Council on Physical Fitness and Sports.

West Virginia

History At-A-Glance

1669
Explorer John Lederer, first European to see western Virginia, reaches top of the Blue Ridge.

c. 1000 B.C.
Mound-building Adena people inhabit the area.

1671
Thomas Batts and Robert Fallam cross Allegheny Mountains to claim Ohio Valley for England.

1600s
Various Native American groups hunt in the region.

1727
Germans from Pennsylvania found New Mecklenburg.

1742
John P. Salling and John Howard find coal on the Coal River.

1754–55
British troops led by George Washington and General Edward Braddock are defeated during French and Indian War.

1773
Plans for the fourteenth colony, which would include West Virginia, fall apart.

1776
Settlers in what is now West Virginia decide they want their own government instead of remaining part of Virginia.

1777–82
British invade the colony three times.

1788
Charleston is founded.

1788
Daniel Boone arrives in Kanawha Valley.

1600   **1700**   **1800**

1492
Christopher Columbus comes to New World.

1607
Capt. John Smith and three ships land on Virginia coast and start first English settlement in New World — Jamestown.

1754–63
French and Indian War.

1773
Boston Tea Party.

1776
Declaration of Independence adopted July 4.

1777
Articles of Confederation adopted by Continental Congress.

1787
U.S. Constitution written.

1812–14
War of 1812.

United States

History At-A-Glance

1836
The Baltimore and Ohio Railroad connects Chesapeake Bay to Harpers Ferry.

1859
Abolitionist John Brown and twenty-one other men raid federal arsenal at Harpers Ferry.

1861
Refusing to leave the Union, western counties of Virginia form the Restored Government of Virginia.

1863
On June 20, West Virginia becomes thirty-fifth state, with Wheeling as capital.

1871
For the first time since Civil War's end, West Virginia's Confederate veterans are allowed to vote.

1907
In an explosion that is the worst mining disaster in U.S. history, 361 die at Monongah.

1913
In Hatfield, mine workers win a nine-hour workday and the right to unionize.

1919–21
Labor disputes involving coal miners, including famous Matewan coal strike of 1920, break out in Logan and Mingo Counties.

1921
First of any state sales tax is introduced.

1959
The National Radio Astronomy Observatory opens at Green Bank.

1968
Seventy-eight die as the result of explosions and fire in a coal mine in Farmington; the disaster leads to new mining safety laws.

1985
Moorefield suffers a major flood.

1800   **1900**   **2000**

1848
Gold discovered in California draws eighty thousand prospectors in the 1849 Gold Rush.

1861–65
Civil War.

1869
Transcontinental railroad completed.

1917–18
U.S. involvement in World War I.

1929
Stock market crash ushers in Great Depression.

1941–45
U.S. involvement in World War II.

1950–53
U.S. fights in the Korean War.

1964–73
U.S. involvement in Vietnam War.

2000
George W. Bush wins the closest presidential election in history.

2001
A terrorist attack in which four hijacked airliners crash into New York City's World Trade Center, the Pentagon, and farmland in western Pennsylvania leaves thousands dead or injured.

▼ **Horseback riders in the 1800s travel in the hills near Moorefield.**

Festivals and Fun for All

Check web site for exact date and directions.

Annual Spring Mountain Heritage Arts and Crafts Festival, Harpers Ferry

For three days during the second full weekend in June, see a variety of arts and crafts and enjoy live bluegrass music, face painting, and other forms of fun. Started in 1969, the festival now attracts tens of thousands of people to Sam Michaels Park each year.
www.jeffersoncounty.com/festival

Autumn Harvest Festival and Road Kill Cookoff, Marlinton

On the last Saturday of September, Marlinton celebrates the harvest with arts and crafts, a parade, soccer games, a classic car show, and a horse show. A road-kill cookoff that challenges chefs to create a disgustingly named dish using an animal commonly found run over on the road is one of the highlights.
www.pocahontascountywv.com

Holiday of Lights, Bluefield

From the end of November to the beginning of January, Bluefield is ablaze with 40 acres (16 ha) of holiday lights, plus horse-drawn wagon rides, Victorian era holiday costumes, Santa, Mrs. Claus, and the elves.
www.ci.bluefield.wv.us

Little Levels Heritage Fair, Hillsboro

During the last full weekend in June, celebrate the birthday of Pearl S. Buck with mountain music and other entertainment, plus local foods. Visit the Sydenstricker House for more fun and a guest speaker sponsored by the Pearl S. Buck Birthplace Foundation.
www.littlelevelsheritagefair.com

Mother's Day Founder Festival, Grafton

On the Saturday before Mother's Day, the birthplace of Anna Jarvis presents an annual quilt auction and selects a Mom-of-the-Year. Other events, such as a Civil War-era fashion show and tea party, vary yearly.
www.annajarvishouse.com

Pioneer Days, Marlinton

Arts and crafts, bluegrass and mountain music, street dances, food, horse-and-buggy rides, and all kinds of old-fashioned fun happen here during the second weekend in July.
www.pocahontascountywv.com

Prickett's Fort State Park, Fairmont

This park offers different living history workshops throughout the year. There is an intense weekend workshop focusing on the skills of early frontier hunters in early Spring. During the third weekend in June, another workshop teaches the many skills of frontier women. A fall weekend seminar teaches the survival and warfare tactics of Native tribes.
www.wvparks.com/prickettsfort

Sue Browning Wildflower Hike, Logan

Since 1987, Chief Logan State Park has been celebrating the beauty of local wildflowers with a one-day hike during the first Saturday in April; prizes and lunch are just part of the fun.
www.chiefloganstatepark.com

Vandalia Gathering, Charleston

Spend Memorial Day weekend celebrating West Virginia's folk heritage with music, dance, storytelling, crafts, quilts, and food, plus competitions for best banjo, fiddle, mandolin, and dulcimer player, and a liar's contest.
www.wvculture.org/vandalia/index.html

West Virginia Days Birthday Celebration, Hinton

During the third weekend in June, see a reenactment of the signing of the West Virginia Statehood proclamation, a historic battle on the streets of Hinton, Union and Confederate camps, Civil War history speakers, and more.
www.netphase.net/~harcc

▶ More than 100,000 people gather annually at the New River Gorge Bridge Day Festival to watch BASE (Building, Antenna, Span, Earth) jumpers leap from the 876 foot (267 m) span and glide to the ground with parachutes. Jumping is allowed only one day each year during the festival.

West Virginia Black Heritage Festival, Clarksburg

The weekend after Labor Day is filled with events that express the black experience. Learn about slavery and the progress made since then, and enjoy soul food, gospel singing, dancing, art, children's games, and more.
Please call (304) 623-2335

West Virginia State Folk Festival, Glenville

Appalachian music, square dancing, storytelling, crafts, fiddle and banjo contests, workshops for aspiring musicians, and a chance to honor citizens who are over seventy highlight this weekend in June.
www.etc4u.com/folkfest

West Virginia Strawberry Festival, Buckhannon

Five days of fun in May celebrate the harvest, including three days of parades, street parties, entertainment, and plenty of ripe, red berries.
www.wvstrawberryfestival.com

MORE ABOUT WEST VIRGINIA

Books

Anderson, Joan Wilkins. *Pioneer Children of Appalachia.* New York: Clarion Books, 1990. Learn how West Virginia's pioneer children lived, worked, dressed, and played.

Bial, Raymond. *Mist Over the Mountains: Appalachia and Its People.* Boston: Houghton Mifflin, 1997. An exciting look at the people and places of West Virginia's mountains.

Tribe, Ivan. *Mountaineer Jamboree: Country Music in West Virginia.* Lexington, KY: University Press of Kentucky, 1996. Learn the history of bluegrass and other music of West Virginia.

Web Sites

▶ Official state web site
www.state.wv.us

▶ Governor's Office
www.wvgov.org

▶ West Virginia Division of Culture and History
www.wvculture.org

▶ Tourism
www.callwva.com

▶ State parks and forests
www. wvparks.com